BANDITS OF TIME

THE LAWS FOR
IMPROVING PERSONAL EFFECTIVENESS

by

Donald E. Simonds, M.Ed.
The Nation's #1 Bounty Hunter

DEDICATION

To Dad who was never late ~

To those who don't have the time to take my
Time Management Seminar ~

and

To those who trusted me to teach their employees ~

ACKNOWLEDGEMENTS

Although I've studied Time Management from the likes of Alec Mackenzie, Alan Lakein, and William Oncken and Donald Wass, the people who taught me the most were the folks I observed.

My father never preached about being on time but always allowed enough time to be early. W.B. Simonds lived by the unspoken motto, "If you're not early, you're late." One of my favorite memories of Dad was when we took him to the train station and he lined his bags along the platform thirty minutes before the train was to arrive.

Bob Muether, my little league baseball coach, had ground rules. In particular, we had to be at the field thirty minutes before game time or we didn't play. I was tardy only once. He sat me on the bench, even though I was the best hitter in the league. Lesson learned.

When I joined SOHIO Petroleum Company, all my colleagues were using the Time Manager International system. Watching them use this comprehensive product encouraged me to follow suit.

Finally, my wife has an incredible attention to detail which makes me better at doing things right the first time, and she insists I not put in too many commas.

Thank you all for the life lessons.

DES
Plano, Texas
July, 2016
www.theentertrainerpro.com

CONTENTS

1

Introduction

OVERVIEW

The objective of this book is to increase your productivity by 25% or the equivalent of two hours per day. This will be accomplished by developing an awareness of what time management is and how it relates to your job. Identifying your personal problem areas and developing strategies for dealing with organizational problems will be the main focus. Additionally, it will be important for you to develop a workable action plan to put these tactics into practice on the job. Finally, you will need a follow-up program to ensure continued effectiveness.

Time management is a misnomer because no one can manage time. You can only manage events throughout the day that might impact the work being done in a timely fashion. Therefore, I consider the definition of time management as, **"Getting results or meeting objectives within limited periods."**

One of the most useful ways of becoming optimally effective is to know what your job is and be able to define it in the fewest number of words. Start by listing the most important aspects of your job. These could be activities, functions, objectives, or specific performance expectations. Then, describe your job in one sentence using the fewest words possible.

For example, "My job is to design and deliver excellent training programs."

Now post that sentence in clear view when working; such as, on your computer monitor or the wall in front of your desk. Read it regularly throughout the day.

2

Bandits of Time

BANDITS DEFINED

The top six universal time wasters are:

1. Not Knowing Where Your Time Goes
    - Working overtime to get things done
    - Don't trust others to get the job done right
    - Feeling overwhelmed and frustrated
    - Saying, "There are not enough hours in the day!"
    - Always functioning under pressure

2. Poor Habits or Lack of Discipline
    - Interfering with work after you have delegated it
    - Saying "Yes" to invitations when you ought to say "No"
    - Welcoming drop-in visitors
    - Responding to the urgent and postponing the important
    - Focusing on the "fun" part of the job

3. Procrastination

- Inability or unwillingness to see that you are putting things off or delaying with false justification

- Thinking "I work best under pressure"

- Fear of mistakes or failure

- Perfectionism

- Fear of reprimand

- Avoiding the unpleasant tasks

4. Handling "Stuff" More Than Once

- Don't recognize that a cluttered desk is a paper blockade

- No system for handling the paper

- Viewed as symbol of busyness or importance

- Can't decide what to do with it

- Don't want to take the time to file it right now

5. Lack of or Inadequate Planning

- Planning limits our freedom

- Crisis oriented

- Action oriented

- Thinking planning never works due to interruptions

- No system

6.   Attempting Too Much

- Desire to multi-task (which has become an epidemic!)
- Unrealistic deadlines
- Responding to the boss' sense of urgency
- Continuous Partial Attention Syndrome
- Desire to appear cooperative

In the next chapter, I will describe my ten Laws for improving your personal effectiveness.

3

The Laws for
Improving Personal Effectiveness

1. THE LAW OF PRECEDENCE

*The right or need to be dealt with first or to
be treated as more important than anybody
or anything else.*

This Law is about setting priorities.   One way to set priorities:

1. List the activities you would like to accomplish today

2. Assign an A, B, or C priority to each activity based upon its importance to your "My job is..." sentence from Chapter 1

    A = Most Important to long term goals, "must" do

    B = Moderately Important to long term goals, "should" do

    C = Least Important, may not have anything to do with long term goals, "like" to do

3. Assign a 1, 2, or 3 priority to each activity based upon its urgency

    1 = Most Urgent in the short term

    2 = Moderately Urgent in the short term

    3 = Least Urgent in the short term

4. Estimate how long each will take

5. Write down the deadline for each item

There is no right way to prioritize. If you just want to use numbers or color code your list, the important thing is to know which items are most important and they are listed in priority order.

2.   THE FIRST LAW OF LIFE

Life is just one boring, routine day after another. Perfect exists only in the imagination.

This Law requires you to design an Ideal Day like the one on the next page:

Morning	
7:00	Drive to work
7:30	Read mail and develop my daily plan
8:00	Work on A #1...
8:30	... uninterrupted for one hour of Intentional Inaccessibility
9:00	Return phone calls & then Start on A #2
9:30	AVAILABLE
10:00	
10:30	
11:00	
11:30	
12:00	Lunch
Afternoon	
12:30	Lunch
1:00	Start on A #3
1:30	AVAILABLE
2:00	
2:30	
3:00	Intentional Inaccessibility for one hour...
3:30	...Start on A #4
4:00	Clean up desk
4:30	Drive home
5:00	
5:30	
6:00	Read novel after dinner

This will give you a target at which to aim. It represents your intention to manage events as effectively as possible.

Next, you'll want to expand the Ideal Day into an Ideal Week. Like this one:

	SUN	MON	TUE	WED	THU	FRI	SAT
Morning							
7:00		Drive to work					
7:30		Read mail and develop my daily plan					
8:00		Work on A #1 uninterrupted for one hour of Intentional Inaccessibility					
8:30							
9:00	Sports Reporters	Staff Mtg. ↓	Return phone calls. Start on A #2. Otherwise, AVAILABLE ↓			Letter Day ↓	Pool Chores ↓
9:30	Walk Dog						
10:00							
10:30							
11:00	Church						
11:30							
Noon	Lunch						
12:30							

	SUN	MON	TUE	WED	THU	FRI	SAT
Afternoon							
1:00							Play
1:30	Family		Start on A #3, if appropriate. Otherwise, AVAILABLE				Golf
2:00	Time						
2:30							
3:00			Intentional Inaccessibility for one hour. Start on A #4, if appropriate.				
3:30							
4:00			Clean up desk				
4:30			Drive home				
5:00							
5:30							
6:00		Read novel after dinner			Do something spontaneous		
6:30							

Notice at 9:00 AM, things change depending upon the day of the week. On Sunday, I like to watch the Sports Reporters for 30 minutes. Monday I have a standing staff meeting. I've allowed an hour and a half, but if we don't need that much time I will use the remainder as I do on Tuesday through Thursday. On Friday, I prepare letters and intend to work on that project until noon. Finally, on Saturday I do pool chores or work in the yard.

Once a student asked me, "Are you really this regimented? Don't you do anything spontaneous?"

I replied, "Absolutely, look at 6:00 PM on Thursday."

This represents my intention to manage the weekly events as effectively as possible.

3.   THE LAW OF THE SCHEMER

Success requires a secret and cunning plan,
especially designed to cause damage or
harm to the Time Bandits.

This Law is about planning and scheduling.   A Daily Planner is a helpful tool in managing yourself. You should use a method that will encourage you to use it. For example, you could use:

- A Personal Digital Assistant
- A desktop program like Outlook Express
- A manual system like a Time Manager ® or Day Timer®

I've used all three types and find the manual system more to my liking.

In order to keep on track, you must have:

A.   A daily plan or "to do" list

B.   A schedule

C.   An appraisal of results

Let's explore each and the three-step processes involved:

   A.   "To Do" List

        1.   List the activities you would like to accomplish today

        2.   Set the priorities (see Law # 1)

        3.   Select up to six items to move to the schedule

One of the potential problems with a "to do" list is it can be demotivating. Imagine you have 25 items on your list. At the end of the day you have only completed five. You think, *Oh my, I still have 20 to go...* that makes you feel bad about how little you accomplished.

Instead, after you have made your list and prioritized it, transfer only the few you think you can realistically accomplish in your day. Usually, that means no more than six.

   B.   Schedule

        1.   Place the Most Important and Most Urgent items on your schedule first. Do the A-1 first, the A-2 second, etc.

        2.   Set aside blocks of time for specific tasks (e.g. 9:00 AM to 10:00 AM – return calls)

        3.   Monitor the activities in relationship to the schedule. Ask yourself, "What is the most important thing to be working on right now?"

I use the term schedule to mean calendar. It is best to have annual, monthly, and daily calendars. Place projects on the annual calendar that are lengthy or in the distant future. Place projects that are weekly or may take longer than a day on your monthly calendar. Place tasks that can be completed today on the daily calendar in a specific time slot (see the Ideal Day).

Think of the plan as what you intend to accomplish and the schedule as your commitment to do it today.

      C.   Appraisal of Results

            1.   List the things on your "To Do" list which you accomplished

            2.   Evaluate their importance relative to your goals and priorities

            3.   Ask, "Could they have been done better? Faster? Simpler? Later? In less detail? By someone else?" etc.

I try to do this as the last activity of the day. It helps me feel a sense of accomplishment and sets up my tomorrow for improvement and success.

4.   THE LAW OF AIMING

The game will be won by hitting the target.

This Law is about setting objectives. To achieve the best results with your work, it will be important to define your work in terms of goals and objectives. Start with a statement of need. For example, "I need to sell more products and services in the coming year."

Next, test the need statement against the following SMART criteria:

Specific-**M**easurable-**A**ttainable-**R**ealistic-**T**ime bound

Specific goals are defined in terms of quality, quantity, timeliness, and cost. Here are some examples of measurement methods for any job:

Area of Measurement	Methods
Quality	* Number of specifications met * % Error rate * % Scrap * Number of complaints received
Quantity	* Number of units produced * Number of units run * Number of calls taken * Sales revenue generated
Timeliness	* % Scheduled dates met * Number of deadlines met * % Within specified timeframes
Cost	* Dollars spent * % Within budget * Dollars of overtime cost

Measurable goals have defined the optimal level. For instance, to produce $500,000 in sales in 12 months is a measurable goal. To improve the image of the organization is not.

Attainable goals are within the capability of the actor. Obviously, if the request is beyond the capacity of the people involved, it's not going to get done. It's important to consider not only your ability but also your willingness to make the change. Any goal that requires somebody to change behavior or improve productivity must encompass both ability and willingness.

Realistic goals are attainable under the current circumstances. You might ask yourself if the goal is attainable under the current budget or other economic constraints of the organization. Is the goal attainable given organizational policy and does it tie into the goals of the department in which you work? Is it realistic to assume you can do the work, given your job description, without usurping the authority of another person?

Time bound means that the goal has clock or calendar constraints. Some goals can be completed within a matter of minutes; others may require a calendar or fiscal year.

In addition to the SMART criteria, your goals should be both challenging and rewarding. Challenging goals require optimal effort on your part. It is inappropriate to have goals that are too easy or too hard. In either extreme, the result is demoralizing. You will rise to the occasion if challenged but won't do well if you feel overwhelmed.

Rewarding goals are ones that incorporate a benefit of accomplishing them. For instance, "If I can figure out a way to get XYZ Company to send its people to us, I'll have a crack at that new assignment I've been after."

The following objective meets the criteria that's just been established:

> "To produce $500,000 in sales revenue in
> 12 months, while keeping returns under
> 2%, closing sales within 45 days, and
> limiting expenses to 4% of revenue."

5. THE LAW OF FINESSE

*To survive, use subtle tricks or deception to
manipulate something or somebody.*

This Law is about managing interruptions. Few things are more frustrating than being interrupted in the middle of your most important project. I've found five important solutions to help avoid interruptions or at least minimize the impact of an interruption. They are:

- Intentional Inaccessibility – If you have an office with a door, close it for one hour (not more than two) so you can concentrate on your most important task. No office? Find a hideout or work from home. Some people are morning people, others are afternoon or evening people; so, book it during peak energy times. Allow interruptions for true emergencies only. Define what that means to your co-workers. For instance, you could say, "Interrupt me if the CEO calls, otherwise no phone calls or visitors."

- Screen Phone Calls and Visitors – If you have a secretary or administrative person to help you, that person should ask the caller or visitor:

  1. What is the purpose of the call? This is necessary in order to get files or other resources available.

  2. How long will it take? This helps determine when the best time would be to handle the issue.

  3. When would the caller be available in the future? Then the assistant can schedule an appointment or call back time that is convenient for both parties.

  4. Offer alternatives. Someone else in the office might be able to handle the issue immediately.

- Evade Distractions – If it is too noisy or you are distracted by something visual; shut your door, rearrange your desk, find a hideout, or work at home.

- Learn to Say "No" – Say it promptly and courteously. I like to say no by saying yes first. For instance, you might say, "I'd love to work on that project. Let me show you why I can't." Then show or explain your priorities. Empathize with the person requesting your time. Perhaps offer an alternative resource who might be available.

- Use a Daily Planner – Plan your availability (see Ideal Day). Plan no more than 80% of your day, which allows a cushion for real emergencies. Evaluate your accomplishments at the end of the day and decide what can be done to improve interruption control for the next day.

6. THE LAW OF PRACTICALITY

If in doubt about what to do next, go home early.

This Law focuses on procrastination. Most of the procrastinators I know are unaware they are doing it. It comes natural to them and they don't recognize the negative impact it has on themselves and others. Here are six ideas to help overcome perpetual procrastination:

- Analyze Where, When, and Why – Procrastination might be triggered by the same stimulus; such as, a particular person, a particular type of task, etc. The first step in lassoing this problem is determining what provokes it. Then discuss the issue with the perpetrator.

- Set Priorities – Write down the things you intend to work on today and focus on the most important (see Law #1).

- Set Realistic Deadlines – This can be tough. We all have a tendency to underestimate how long a task will take. Guess how long you think it will take to complete the project then add at least a 20% safeguard. Track your estimates to develop your accuracy.

- Don't Avoid the Unpleasant – It's human nature to postpone an unpleasant duty like calling an angry client. Instead of ducking the unpleasant or difficult, do it first and get it out of the way.

- Escape Perfectionism – The perfectionists I know don't believe this is a problem and if your boss is one, oh my. In reality, perfection doesn't exist (see Law #2). Don't allow perfectionism to paralyze you. Break a large project down into smaller, bite-sized pieces.

- Practice Task Completion – Starting and stopping work on a project is just as bad on your efficiency as frequent starts and stops are on a car's gas mileage.

7. THE LAW OF SPATIAL ARRANGEMENT

One must always arrange the work
components in a way that creates a
particular structure.

Since this is my biggest problem, I know how easy it is to get out of hand. This Law will help with personal disorganization, dealing with the paperwork, and distracting clutter. When I'm at my best, I follow these simple rules:

- Practice Task Completion – There are three simple rules. You might even post them on a wall chart if this is your main concern:

  1. Clear your desk of everything except the one thing you are working on at the moment

  2. Finish it

  3. Put it away

- File When Done – No exceptions! Only file papers which you would be unable to get elsewhere. Learn how to file. If you think that sounds ludicrous then you probably don't know there is a science to filing.

- Take All Possible Action – There are basically four options when dealing with the paper flow (see Law #8). They are:

1. Dump it in the trash if it is not something that requires your action

2. Delegate it to the appropriate person for action

3. Do it now, if it can be done in a relatively short period of time

4. Delay it to a more appropriate time. This may require putting it in a project file, tickler file, or placing a note on your schedule.

- Send It on Its Way – See the above choices but get it off your desk.

- Create a Corridor – At the end of the work day, everything should be off your desk. This practice produces a mental break between work and home, reduces stress, and increases energy for the next day. There is nothing better than to arrive at work to a clean desk.

8. THE LAW OF ALLIGATORS

When you're up to your elbows in alligators,
drain the swamp.

Paperwork can be daunting. Decisiveness is the key. There are only four choices:

1. Dump it – Ask yourself, "Is this something that requires action?" If the answer is no, throw it in the trash. If the answer is yes, go to question 2.

2. Do it – Ask yourself, "Is this something *I must do*?" If the answer is no, go to question 3. If the answer is yes, ask, "Should it be done now, in the time I have available?" If the answer is yes, do it and file it. If the answer is no, go to question 4.

3. Delegate it – Ask yourself, "Whose responsibility is this?" Then, write that person's name on it and drop it in the out box.

4. Defer it – Ask yourself, "When should this be done?" Then, make a note on the calendar page as a reminder and file it in the appropriate place.

9.   THE LAW OF PURSUIT

*If pursued, don't circle the wagons – circle
the pursuers.*

This Law deals with over-commitment, which can be the result of wanting to please everyone. The obvious solution is to learn to say "No." Say it logically, firmly, and tactfully (if possible), but say it.

Learning to say "No" can apply to different problem areas, as you saw in Law #5. If more appropriate, offer an alternative; such as, the availability of a co-worker or renegotiate priorities.

This Law also deals with working on the right things. Efficiency is doing things right; effectiveness is doing the right things.

Vilfredo Pareto, a nineteenth-century Italian economist, noticed that 80% of the wealth in Italy was held by 20% of the people. He then hypothesized that the significant items in any given group would constitute a relatively small portion of the total (the Pareto Principle).

Joseph Juran was the first to use the terms "vital few" and "trivial many" in applying the Pareto Principle to a great variety of management situations. For instance, 80% of your headaches are caused by 20% of the staff. Twenty percent of the inventory represents 80% of the value.

It doesn't have to be exactly 80% either. An insurance company found that 10% of its accounts represented 90% of its sales value. In his book, *The 80/20 Principle,* Richard Koch says, "the 80/20 rule is a convenient metaphor for a pattern of imbalance... It may be 65/35, 75/25, 95/5... It doesn't even have to add up to 100. It could be that 80% of your revenue comes from 30% of your products."

The point is that you need not do everything. You've got to decided what activities are going to give you the 80% of your results.

Refusing to do the unimportant is a requisite for success. Too often people work on administrative tasks that are unnecessary or irrelevant with respect to their goals and objectives. If you want to get more done or exceed your expectations, follow this simple rule:

> Have the goal visible and when you start an activity ask, "*Is this going to help me achieve my goal?*" If the answer is "No", then don't do it. This focuses your attention on the vital few not the trivial many.

10. THE LAW OF BITTER FRUIT

*To determine why the tree bore bitter fruit,
examine what might have poisoned its roots.*

The emphasis of this Law is problem-solving. The following are steps which eliminate or control your personal problem areas.

    1.   Analyze the Present

        A.   Take an Activity Inventory

            1.   Prepare a daily to-do list, assign priorities (see Law #1), and a deadline.

            2.   Record everything you do during the day. That means everything. If you are interrupted, note the source and reason in detail.

3.   Document the duration, priority, and your feelings about the impact of this activity on your day/time.

See the sample "Activity Inventory" on the next page.

Example:

Activity Inventory

Name: *Don Simonds*   Date: *10/01/XXXX*

Daily Plan:

1. Do LIMRA for Harold A1 by 9 A	4. Prep confirmation letters A2 b4 5 P
2. Prepare to interview Ron A1 by 1 P	5. Contact Jan Allen B2 at 3 P
3. Prepare for Staff Meeting B1 by 9 A	6. Call warm nominees B2 fit in

Time	Activity	Duration	Priority	Notes
8:15	*Copied handouts for staff meeting*	*Minutes 15*	B	*Good use of time while waiting for Harold to arrive*
8:30	*Moved stuff out of my office*	*8*	C	*Enables Harold to work un-interrupted on his LIMRA*
8:38	*Read Franklin Covey catalogue*	*22*	C	*Not important but fun*
9:00	*Read Ron's resume*	*12*	A	*Preparing for Ron's interview*
9:12	*Set up Harold on LIMRA*	*5*	A	*#1 goal of the day*
9:17	*Requested FARA score on self & running dummy rate quotes*	*30*	A	*Helps me learn the system & answer questions of applicants*
9:47	*Continued looking through Covey*	*53*	C	*Killing time waiting on Harold to finish LIMRA*
10:40	*Interrupted by Bill*	*10*	*Lower than C*	*Total waste of my time socializing*
10:50	*Met with Harold to debrief and discuss next steps*	*15*	A	*#1 goal of the day completed* **Yea!**

B.   Analyze and Define the Problem

1.   What went right each day? Why?

2.   What went wrong each day? Why?

3.   What time did you start on your top priority task? Why? Could you have started it earlier?

4.   Did you spend the first hour of your day well, doing important things?

5.   What was the most productive period of your day? Why?

6.   What was the least productive period of your day? Why?

7.   What accounted for most of your interruptions?

8.   What were the reasons for the interruptions?

9.   How much of your time was spent on high value activity?

10. How much of your time was spent on low value activity?

11. What did you do today that could have been eliminated?

12. What activities could you spend less time on and still obtain acceptable results?

13. What activities needed more time today?

14. What activities could be delegated? To Whom?

15. What patterns and habits are apparent from your Activity Inventory?

2. Determine Causes of the Problem

    A. List possible causes of the problem

        1. Brainstorm at least 5 causes

        2. Answer the question "why?" 5 times

    B. Look for patterns

    C. Determine most probable or most costly cause

3. Develop a List of Solution Alternatives

    A. Think about desired results

    B. What resources are available

    C. Are there any conditional limitations?

    D. Brainstorm available alternatives

See the sample "Cause-Solution Worksheet" on the next page.

Example:

Cause - Solution Worksheet

Problem and Cost (Time/$)	Causes	Solutions
Telephone 30-60 minutes per day	a. Have no plan for handling	a. Incoming - develop a plan for screening and delegating. Outgoing - consolidate and inform.
	b. Have a desire to be available	b. Distinguish between business and pleasure
	c. "Answer your own" policy or desire	c. Recognize the waste of time – delegate don't assume legitimacy
	d. Over-dependent staff	d. Refuse to make their decisions – encourage initiative – allow mistakes
	e. Inability to terminate calls	e. Learn and practice closing techniques * be candid * foreshadow ending * hang-up on self * preset time limits

4. Develop a Plan to Improve

    A.   Set goals

    B.   Develop objectives

    C.   List activities and timeframes

    D.   Select resources

    E.   Describe barriers and contingency plans

    F.   Make a commitment

See the sample "Action Plan" on the next page.

Action Plan

Instructions:

- **Goal** – Make a broad statement about what you want to accomplish
- **Objectives** – Specific, Measurable, Attainable, Realistic, and Time bound accomplishments needed to reach your goal
- **Activities/Time** – "To Do" items needed to reach the objectives
- **Resources** – Include people, money, equipment, facilities, etc.
- **Barriers/Contingencies** – List potential problems and how to prevent them
- **Commitment** – Whose support will you need and how will you obtain it?

Example:

- **Goal** – Practice Intentional Inaccessibility
- **Objectives** – Develop habit of 1 hour of Intentional Inaccessibility by 8/15/xx. Train staff to handle visitors, phone, etc. by 8/1/xx
- **Activities/Time** – Discuss plans with boss, tomorrow. Meet with staff to explain action plan after boss' approval. Set-up schedule with each for a one-on-one for Thursday
- **Resources** – Staff and boss
- **Barriers/Contingencies** – Real emergency during Intentional Inaccessibility – Define emergency – Continue after emergency or next day
- **Commitment** – I pledge to do this activity for 30 days without exception and to evaluate results. Need support from staff and boss

4

Enforcing the Laws

TIME MASTERY

Time mastery requires changing habits and attitudes. First you must want to change. When someone says, "I don't have the time …", the subtext is, "It's not that important to me."

Personal motivation is based upon desires, self-evident profitability, and pay value. The payoff must be large enough for you to want to do the work required to implement and maintain the new habit. Seeing the reward leads to self-starting, accepting accountability, increased drive and energy, and commitment to change.

Once you have made the commitment to the change, then you'll want to follow these steps to eliminate and replace ineffective habits with new ones:

1. Analyze your Activity Inventory and decide what needs to change

2. Develop a Plan to Improve (see previous page)

3. Post reminders; such as, your Ideal Day

4. Be committed to the new habit for thirty days

5. Tell others what you are doing and ask for support

CREATE THE RIGHT ATTITUDE

Attitudes are based upon your belief system; the assumptions, concepts, values, and practices that constitute the way you view reality. If you believe you can't do something, you won't even try. It's impossible to bring about meaningful change if you do nothing.

The key to controlling your attitude is to control your self-talk. What you think is critical, what you affirm will happen. Here are some guidelines for creating your affirmations:

1. They need to be personal – Affirm what is right for you. Write each as an "I" statement.

2. Always use positive language – Describe the positive result not what you are trying to correct.

3. State them in present tense – Assume the change has happened already, not "someday."

4. Describe achievement of the goal or habit – Write "I am" or "I have" not "I will."

5. Avoid comparisons – Affirm what is right for you not "I'm as good as William Goldman."

6. Use action words – "I enjoy," "I love to," "I show," "I feel," etc.

7. Use excitement words – Use words that spark an emotional picture like "I happily."

8. Be truthful – Affirm what you can honestly imagine yourself becoming.

9. Balance – Strive for growth in all areas of your life.

10. Realistic – Perfection is self-defeating. Avoid "I always," or "I'll never."

11. Private – Your affirmations are for your eyes only.

Examples:

I easily keep my filing up-to-date so that information can be quickly found.

I am an action person. I do first things first and one thing at a time.

It's fun and easy to be organized.

I have a positive expectancy of reaching my goals and I vividly know my plan of attack.

I manage meetings professionally. My meetings are complete, well timed, and dynamic.

I am logical and decisive in making important decisions.

I am Pygmalion to myself and to all my employees.

I don't have to do anything. I want to, I choose to, I like it, it's my idea.

Guidelines for Imprinting

To achieve your goals, imagination is almost as important as the work. Imprinting helps lead you toward your goals. You can't win the prize if you don't see it. Here are the steps to imprinting:

A.   Read the affirmation aloud or silently, whichever you prefer

B.   Imagine your future so vividly it seems as if you've already lived it and it is a memory

C.   Feel the emotion of accomplishment

Repeat the process at least twice each day.

DAILY PRIORITIES

In the overview, I suggested you describe your job in one sentence. This is mine, "My job is to design and deliver excellent training programs."

This is critical to getting your priorities straight. Every morning when you are prioritizing your "To Do" list, ask yourself, "Does this have anything to do with 'My job is ....'?" If it does, then it should probably be an A priority. If not, then it is a B or C priority.

You can also use this sentence as a deciding factor in when to say "No." If someone asks you to do something, ask, "Does this have anything to do with 'My job is ....'?" If not, say "No."

Use Señor Pareto's rule to help prioritize. If the task will not help you get the 80% of your results, don't give it a high priority. Also, consider doing the highest priority work during your Intentional Inaccessibility hour(s). Let's assume you work an 8-hour day. What is 20% of 8 hours? 1.6 hours. Right? So, if you set aside two hours per day when you can work totally uninterrupted, you should be able to get nearly all of your A priorities finished.

DAILY PLANNING AND SCHEDULING

Planning and scheduling go hand-in-hand. Planning means thinking about what you want to do. It equates to your intentions to accomplish your goals. Scheduling means placing a specific task on your calendar, determining the time in which you will work on the task. It equates to a commitment to take action during that timeframe.

Your Ideal Day will give you a target at which to aim. It represents your intention to manage events as effectively as possible, but it only becomes a commitment when you slot in your A #1 task on your calendar.

Similarly, the Ideal Week represents your intention to manage the weekly events as effectively as possible, but it only becomes a commitment when you slot in the specifics of that project with a deadline.

BALANCE GOALS AND OBJECTIVES

Time management is really about managing events or yourself with respect to getting results or meeting objectives.

Your self-management begins with defining performance clearly. Most jobs can be realistically described within the framework of three to seven functional areas called Performance Results Categories (PRCs).

For example: A sales person might be evaluated on how well she:

A. Manages the assigned territory

B. Acquires new accounts or the associated sales volume

C. Satisfies customers

D. Develops product knowledge

E. Maintains inter-departmental relations

Therefore, you should have long-range goals for each PRC. These long-range goals should be written down and read every day. You might want to include them in your affirmations.

The next step is to identify your SMART objectives. You will want to generate a list of alternatives. The list should include two or three ways of accomplishing each PRC.

Example alternatives for our sales person might be:

- To produce $500,000 in sales revenue in 12 months

- To acquire three new accounts per quarter

- To balance product mix across all lines by year-end

The following objective includes all four measurement criteria established (see Law #4):

> To produce $500,000 in sales revenue in 12 months, while keeping returns under 2%, closing sales within 45 days, and limiting expenses to 4% of revenue.

Additionally, managing your personal productivity and achieving your desired outcomes is contingent on how you behave. Not only do you need to know what the performance expectation is, you need to think about the skills or actions that will be needed to achieve it.

People often fail to make the desired behavior a part of the SMART objectives. By determining the means to attaining the desired result, you will increase your probability of success.

If our sales person is going to reach the target of $500,000 in sales revenue, she will have to call a certain number of prospects, qualify leads, articulate customer needs, demonstrate capability to satisfy those needs, write proposals, negotiate deliverables, etc.

How will she find the time? She will need to write down the Behavioral Objectives and include them in her Daily Planner.

Example:

SMART Objectives	Behavioral Objectives
To produce $500,000 in sales revenue in 12 months, while keeping returns under 2%, closing sales within 45 days, and limiting expenses to 4% of revenue.	• Initiate 10 phone calls per day • Schedule 20 face-to-face calls per month • Write two proposals per week

Finally, it's important to have balanced goals. This means creating goals and objectives in all areas of your life. Such as:

- Family
- Career
- Spiritual
- Social
- Financial
- Health and Wellness
- Personal Development
- Leisure Time

You might also write affirmations in all these areas as well.

HANDLE INTERRUPTIONS

Analyze the situations in which you are interrupted. Who interrupts the most? When does it occur in clock or calendar time? What is the duration of each? Is there a pattern? If you are always interrupted by the same person, you can confront the person and work out a solution.

You might also use the Activity Inventory as a tool. One day when I first started tracking my activities, a colleague came in and sat down. I knew that the topic of discussion was likely to be the Houston Astros. Before he began, I said, "Just one second." I turned to my Activity Inventory and as I wrote on it I said, "Nine-fifteen, Leland Charles." I then turned toward him and said, "Go." As you probably guessed, he said, "What are you doing?" I said, "I'm tracking my activities to see where I waste time." He got up and left. He never came back to socialize again (see how not to offend your co-workers below). I thought that was a great learning moment and have been using the technique ever since. I also use it with telephone interruptions.

Another technique is to suggest alternatives. For instance, I love baseball and wouldn't have minded talking about the Astros with Leland. The problem was I was busy and didn't need to be interrupted. So, I might have said, "Why don't we have lunch together and chat about last night's game."

If the interruption is about business, you could suggest scheduling an appointment for another time. You might say, "I'm under a deadline, can we meet later today? How's three o'clock for you? How much time do we need?" That way you will be able to finish your work and you haven't offended your coworker. Furthermore, your associates will start learning to make appointments.

ELIMINATE PROCRASTINATION

The most important issue here is awareness. Analyze the situations in which you procrastinate. Is there a pattern? If you tend to miss deadlines involving the same type of work, or with the same people, you can figure out the root cause and work out a solution.

Perhaps the best solution is to delegate (see next section) the task to someone who might enjoy it. If that is not possible, then set priorities and schedule the time to do what must get done. No excuses!

Often people procrastinate because the work is not fun. The busy work or paperwork (doing an expense report) gets postponed. When I traveled 25-30 weeks a year, I always did my expense reports first thing the morning following the trip. I knew if I postponed the task, it would delay my getting reimbursed. Give yourself a reward for doing the unpleasant tasks.

DELEGATE EFFECTIVELY

Delegating is the transfer of a specific job, function, or task from you to another. It requires determining three things:

1.   Responsibility
2.   Accountability
3.   Authority

Responsibility pertains to the task or assignment to be delegated. You should not just dump work you don't want to do. Find someone for which this would be an upgrade in duties, an opportunity to learn a new skill, or an enjoyable change of pace.

Accountability requires you to outline the specific guidelines for the assignment and to describe the obligation in terms of:

- Quality (acceptable number of errors permitted or rework)
- Quantity (number of products or services produced)
- Timeliness (milestones or deadlines)
- Cost (budget)

Most importantly, delegating also involves deciding upon a level of decision-making authority based upon the employee's willingness and ability.

If the delegate is a beginner in the job and not feeling confident or competent, provide specific instructions.

When the delegate has had some success and willingness is obvious but ability may be low, you should use a coaching style to influence the decisions.

After a person's ability is clear, use a consulting style to increase the employee's willingness to assume responsibility.

Finally, once the employee is performing at a high achiever level, you may simply state the objectives of the task and allow the employee to figure out how, when, and what is necessary.

DEAL WITH WRITTEN COMMUNICATION

To master this issue, you must master your world first. We receive letters, e-mails, job descriptions, proposals, reports, presentations, etc.

Create a workflow process and create a habit. You might need to post the workflow in an easily visible space. Pick up the paper or open the e-mail and ask every time:

1. What is this? Is it related to my top priorities?

2. Is it my responsibility? If not, dump it or send it to the appropriate person.

3. If yes, should I do it now or defer it?

Practicing Task Completion is the single most important method for dealing with the written communication problem.

IMPROVE MEETINGS

If meetings are your nightmare, make sure you follow these guidelines:

1.   Always prepare and post desired outcomes, ground rules, and an agenda which are visible to all.

2.   Start on time even if someone is tardy, no exceptions.

3.   Stick to the agenda, avoid going off on tangents, and allow attendance as needed.

4.   Record all decisions and use a scribe for listing discussion points on a white board or flip chart visible to all.

5.   Hold stand-up meetings for announcements. Once people sit down, meetings take longer.

6.   End each meeting with an evaluation. Ask participants what worked well and what might be changed with regard to both the results and the process.

7.   Send out the meeting minutes within 24 hours. Include all decisions and specific assignments of *who* will do *what* by *when*. There is nothing worse than having someone say, "I didn't know I was supposed to do that." Put it in writing.

INVOLVE THE TEAM

Once you have developed a plan to attack your Time Bandits, let the staff know about them. For example, if you intend to be inaccessible for one or two hours per day, you need to explain your intentions and ask your team for support. Define what an emergency is and ask not to be disturbed unless that happens.

Lead by example even if you are not technically a supervisor. Others will learn good habits from you when they see you practicing good habits; such as, starting meetings on time, every time.

Ask others how you waste their time and seek suggestions on how to correct the problems. Then get out of the way.

Finally, make time management a topic for staff meetings. Ask everyone for ideas on how to improve the team's use of time.

5

Putting the Bandits Away for Life

ANALYZE REGULARLY

Old habits die hard. In order to put these Bandits away for life, you'll need to keep at it.

I recommend that you take an Activity Inventory on a regular basis. Some do it semi-annually, others quarterly, or monthly. I'm at my best when I do it continuously. Use it as a tool (see Handle Interruptions in Chapter 4).

When you analyze the results, keep in mind there are only four reasons for success or failure:

> **Coincidental Factors** – Anything outside your control that helped or hindered in accomplishing the desired result.

> **The SMART Objective** – Sometimes the performance expected isn't realistic, clear, or controllable. Sometimes you may want to

raise the bar to increase the expectation and challenge yourself to greater performance.

Actions or Skills Used – Performance targets could have been met due to the actions you took. If not met, there may have been skills you have that weren't used, or there may be skills you need to be trained to use.

The Boss' Behavior – The manager may have done something that helped or hindered performance.

Once you know the root cause, adjust your plan accordingly to do better next time. Through incremental change, you'll become more and more proficient.

DURING THE FIRST MONTH

Evaluate the top three Time Bandits from your analysis. Complete a Cause-Solution Worksheet and develop an Action Plan for each one. Don't try to work on more than three during the first month.

Discuss your Action Plans with your work group so there are no surprises.

Use a Daily Planner, develop an Ideal Day, and an Ideal Week. Post them in a convenient place to help you remember your intentions.

You might want to read another book on this subject. Some of my favorites are listed in the Bibliography.

Review your progress at the end of the month. Note any additional actions needed to control your top three Bandits. Repeat the process for the next three Bandits.

Schedule bi-weekly progress meetings with your team if any of them are involved.

TWO MONTHS LATER

Review your progress at the end of the second month. Note any additional actions needed to control Bandits four through six. Repeat the process for Bandits seven through ten.

THREE MONTHS LATER

Take another Activity Inventory at the end of the third month. Estimate productivity gains. If you are not satisfied with your progress, identify areas that need improvement and develop solutions and Action Plans to resolve the issues.

LONG RANGE

Schedule Activity Inventories semi-annually, quarterly, or as frequently as you need to keep the momentum going.

Evaluate progress, problems, and plans quarterly.

Establish a reinforcement program based upon your learning style. This could include developing a reading list of books and articles, checking out films on specific trouble areas, looking for audio programs, or hiring me for a live event or personal coaching.

Best wishes for your success!

BIBLIOGRAPHY

Allen, David, *Getting Things Done; The Art of Stress-Free Productivity* (New York: Viking, 2001).

Davis, Brian L. et. al. *Successful Manager's Handbook* (Minneapolis: Personnel Decisions, Inc., 1989).

Drucker, Peter F., *The Effective Executive* (New York: Harper & Row, 1966).

Drucker, Peter F. *Managing for Results* (New York: HarperBusiness, 1986).

Doyle, Michael and Straus, David *How to Make Meetings Work* (New York: Jove Books, 1976).

Fisher, R., & Ury, W. *Getting to Yes: Negotiating Agreement Without Giving In.* (New York: Penguin Books, 1981).

Goleman, Daniel *Emotional Intelligence: Why It Can Matter More Than IQ* (New York: Bantam Books, 1995).

Heller, Robert and Hindle, Tim *Essential Manager's Manual* (New York: DK Publishing, Inc., 1998).

Huszczo, Gregory E. *Tools for Team Leadership* (Palo Alto: Davies-Black Publishing, 2004).

Imai, Masaaki *Kaizen* (New York: McGraw-Hill, 1986).

Jones, Curtis H., "The Money Value of Time" Harvard Business Review, July-August, 1968, pp. 94-101.

Kepner, Charles H., and Tregoe, Benjamin B., *The Rational Manager* (New Jersey: Kepner- Tregoe, Inc., 1965).

Lehmkuhl, Dorothy and Lamping, Dolores, *Organizing for the Creative Person* (New York: Three Rivers Press, 1993).

Lencioni, Patrick *The FIVE Dysfunctions of a TEAM* (San Francisco: Jossey-Bass, 2002).

Lakein, Alan, *How to Get Control of Your Time and Your Life* (New York: Peter H. Wyden, 1973).

Mackenzie, Alec, *The Time Trap*; The New Version (New York: AMA, 1990).

Mackenzie, R. Alec, *The Time Trap* (New York: AMA, 1972).

Moore, Leo B., "Managerial Time", Industrial Management Review, Spring, 1968, pp. 77-85.

Oncken, William Jr. and Wass, Donald L., "Management Time: Who's Got the Monkey?" Harvard Business Review, November-December, 1974, pp. 75-80.

Plunkett, Lorne C. and Hale, Guy A., *The Proactive Manager* (New York: John Wiley & Sons, 1982).

Simonds, Donald E., *Achieving on Purpose: Your GUIDE to Managerial Success* (Publisher: Author, 2014)

Smith, Hyrum W. *The 10 Natural Laws of Successful Time and Life Management: Proven Strategies for increased Productivity and Inner Peace* (New York: Warner Books, 1994).

Tichy, Noel M. and Bennis, Warren G. *JUDGMENT* (New York: Penguin Group, 2007).

Tracy, Brian *Time Power: A Proven System for Getting More Done in Less Time Than You Ever Thought Possible* (New York: AMACOM, 2007).

Tyler, Chaplin, "Steps in Becoming a Better Manager", Chemical Engineering, April 30, 1962, pp. 105-108.

Winston, Stephanie, *Getting Organized* (New York: Warner Books, 1978).